The Phenix City Story, Bertha's Confession

LAMURIEL YVONNE OJO

The Phenix City Story, Bertha's Confession

ISBN: 978-0-9855978-3-2

CONTENTS

INTRODUCTION

A GLISTENING LIGHT FLICKERED in the tunnel of darkness; can success be more than a pin point from afar?

Desiring not to quit by judging the distance ahead, I fight the thought that joy is impossible.

My great aunt use to say, "Life gives off flavors that can either be inviting with pleasant tastes; like a peach cobbler bubbling inside the oven, cinnamon sugar and vanilla flavor floating through the nose hairs tickling with every sniff, or unappealing like grimy chitterlings-unseasoned and thrown in the cast iron black pot. All served up on the plate with no hot sauce in sight-just bland and gritty with many mystery tongue tying ingredients,

You're just doggone unprepared with every bite!"

Bertha was the luscious, vivacious diva, contributing to the buzz for Phenix City, Alabama. The buzz is the gossip and happenings of the town. These pages relay the story about her transformation from being the daily popular beauty that pleased the crowd to a Christ- centered individual, caring about the purpose and will of God.

Phenix City is the county seat of Russell County and is located in east Alabama along the west bank of the Chattahoochee River. This small city previously known as Girard, became notorious during the 1940s and 1950s for being a haven to organized crime of gambling, narcotics, and prostitution. Customers came from surrounding rural areas and neighboring military towns to enjoy the allowable activity renowned by Phenix City. Those dangerous good times were no stranger to Bertha. The streets were a part of her life at a young age. Now she was in her middle adult years and continuing to enjoy sin without question.

We all have made decisions that lead to mistakes and regrets at some point and time in our life span. All has fallen short in our walk after the Glory of God. The end goal is to realize when we are on the wrong path, U-turn, come to the purpose, and will of God the Father, Son, and Holy Spirit.

"And do not be conformed to this world, but be transformed by the renewing of your mind, that you may prove what *is* that good and acceptable and perfect will of God (Romans 12:2,3)."

This book is for the one who has messed up and looking to make a mark for Jesus Christ after realizing the stumble or even worse the fall into a sinful lifestyle. This book of testimony is for that youth and young teen who think the world's temptations are irresistible, and popularity and people pleasing are worth the sacrifice of his or her soul.

All actions good or bad impact life and my prayer is after reading The Phenix City Story the hope of creating a buzz for the maker, our creator will spur your discernment and decisions of life along a more fruitful path.

Be blessed as you read.

LaMuriel Yvonne Ojo
mirrorbuzz99@gmail.com

CHAPTER 1

Light

"You are the light of the world. A town built on a hill cannot be hidden. Neither do people light a lamp and put it under a bowl. Instead they put it on its stand, and it gives light to everyone in the house.

Mt 5:14-15

BERTHA WAS THE belle of the town in South Phenix City, Alabama. The population according to the United States Census Bureau in the year of 1980 was around 20,000.

Bertha knew about half of those people during the period of my preteen days. As I watched her fashion flair, observed her quirks and expressions with the slow tenor drawl, my desire was to be popular just like her. She just did not appear anywhere in town unrecognized. A local celebrity, sophisticated and stylish with dark chocolate skin, brown eyes, perfect white teeth including a fourteen carat gold tooth with a star in the front. And that velvety tenor voice seems to bring everyone under a spell.

She stood about 5"6 with a pear like build, narrow shoulders, along with small waist and busty curvy hips that she swung freely in stacks showing her long smooth stallion calves. She had pencil length thick dark hair that laid in curled perfection daily by the hot irons. Everybody was joyously greeted with her flippant "Hey dahling" and welcomed it.

Aunt Bertha was boisterous, good at pleasing the people. She had a history of being promiscuous, partying hard until the sun set is up in the sky. She was notorious for putting others in their proper position with words or, if necessary, escalating to a back hand with a quick cross fist if they did not show the proper respect.

I knew her in later years when most reported a slumber in her wild, outlandish street ways. Repeatedly it was proclaimed to us young tenderoni's in the family, that the present aunt was the saved 50-year-old.

Mom felt otherwise. "Your Aunt Bertha continues to hold to habits I don't approve of. You are not allowed to go there unless I am around and your dad knows this."

Of course, Dad has his own personal mind set about family. He also practiced familiar habits. Often we would venture onto Aunt Bertha's without mom knowing. It was usually early Saturday afternoons when mom would go to work. Sometimes we thought we was going to see

Dad's sister Dessa "the good aunt," who lived a quarter of a mile down the road on the opposite side of the street.

Dad's mom, Grandma Rena, and his sister were so close they almost acquired the same address number. Grandma Rena's was 1226 9th avenue and Aunt Dessa's was 226 Seale Road. Grandma did not like Aunt Bertha's close relationship with dad or Aunt Dessa. Nor that she lived less than a quarter mile from her and visited her often. Aunt Bertha clearly made her skin crawl whether she was family or not.

Later, I discovered there were sour history with Aunt Bertha and Grandma Rena. It was very hush hush. No one would give specifics, only blank stares and change the subject. I kept asking until the memorable day my feet dangled five inches off the ground by rugged caveman hands jerking my shirt. Oddly enough an uncle's face hovered through the thick bristled hairs falling on my smooth facial skin and spayed my innocence with liquorish saliva rain. It entered directly into my eyeballs as he yelled...

> "Stop being nosey, you hear ..." "Shut-up, and don't ask again!"

I did not desire a second splatter of smelly liquor laced onion mouth juice. Sprinting away, my thought was I do not care to ever know.

Aunt Dessa was a favorite. My sister and I often visited her house. She was an avid church goer, but the pots were never as full along with the electric sounds of excitement as Aunt Bertha's. Her home did not spark with eclectic friends, dancing to blues and Motown songs.

Absent were the smoke filled rooms from odd looking cigarettes, snickering joined by cursing jokes and pokes being passed. And then the conversations overheard were often packed with grown up talk about men. My sister and I could hear everything through the paper thin walls, and you must believe we kept it in our memory. On those visits I was more than educated about a man's anatomy and what was done with it.

One Sunday after church I went to Grandma's place. Her house was not too far from the 13th street Bridge and 9th Avenue. My sister, cousin and I liked playing at the federal bank across the street with the huge paved parking lot. It was great for riding bike, running and ball play or just snooping and watching the sites. This time after service it was just Grandma Rena and me. And she was in a mood for reminiscing old times. Church service was long, but good along with the fatty dinner of fried chicken and okra, soft butter biscuits and freshly churned vanilla ice cream.

"Grandma, why don't Aunt Bertha come around here much?"

"Oh, she won't ever step foot in this house here, let me tell yah!" I giggled as she went on.

Your Aunt Bertha would hang in the streets with your Dad and aunt and trouble would find them, from the late night club brawls, dented front car hoods after car chasing, to the jail house. She invited trouble and knew every pimp in town it seemed. I got your dad out of jail three times because of her!"

Grandma murmured as she pointed her finger toward me, "Just because she is older don't mean she is better, and a feisty, young speckled cat that gets older isn't anything but an older, slow moving speckled cat. It don't lose its specks, and show don't change its ways."

"Yes ma'am."

I understood her words to mean, Aunt Bertha was doing the same old things in her old age as when she was younger. She was just slower at moving because of those extra forty- fifty pounds. Oddly I could not imagine Aunt Bertha being slow at anything, even with the added poundage. She would welcome the neighborhood rat and make him bow with her pitchy "Hey dahling," "You look good girl!" "Come talk to me, baby," or "What you bring this momma, sweetie?" Never once did I recall anyone getting past her eyesight unwelcomed. Drinking and eating flowed in abundance in her presence.

Maybe Momma Rena could honestly admit that Aunt Bertha cooled down her outlandish ways. Fewer in the number were the hosted parties or street sweeps after midnight as she aged. I often imagined during the family gossip, her stepping with silver_stiletto's, black gripping leather pants and a red and white bustier through some floozy joints' front door or blue_lights in the basement party crying "Hello darlings!" Circular multi-colored lights bouncing off the walls, voices resounding in unison, "She's here, the party queen, let's Boogie!"

Reality checked in at the belch of strawberry soda. My throat released the appropriate words grandma expected, "Yes ma'am, I understand."

The Unwanted Visitor

The routine five to six times a year when Aunt Bertha was around, whether we went to her or she came to you included a "Come here dahling and give your auntie some sugar."

The kisses would land wet and hard on your cheek or directly on the lips. My sister and I would attempt to hide our disgust by smiling, when released, our sprint was to the nearest bathroom for a facial scrub and splatter. But her kisses were tolerable for the dollars your pocket would receive after leaving. That, of course, made everything better.

On occasion big paper money was shared after coercing it from "uncle" (whatever man she was with at that time). Aunt Bertha musical_A flat shrieks could make your toes curl gratefully when demanding action.

"Give my babies some money. Don't be so cheap (when they pull out pocket change) or you will pay later on. I mean get that wallet out now!"

We smirked. Our right hand itching as the money came jingling out if it was coins. The smiles flipped to big toothy grins if ten's or twenties rolled from the fingers.

"Thank you, Auntie," we would chime in perfect harmony as we lit out the back door to the candy store with permission.

One particular visit stood out in memory. The room was a thick gray haze from cigarettes of all types. Teddy Pendergrass was playing in the background on the record player. It was the summer of 1980. Aunt Bertha cooked collard greens, black eyed peas, chicken dressing and pig's feet, and Dad stopped by to eat. She could make a pot sing and later you would suck the juice from your fingers in delight. Her specialty was potato salad and pound cake, included with all of which decorated the long maple wood table walking in the kitchen.

Men and women were sitting around the house. An unfolded blue card table set up in the front room, money filled the center. Blank stares with straight lips or scowls hid behind raised cards. Beer cans and short glasses lined up along the sides of the table along with ashtrays with cigarette butts. Later I found out those short glasses contained gin or bourbon most times. We walked in the murky room with the blinds still half closed, but the back door open wide to let air through the screen.

Auntie immediately resounded, "Hello Larry dahling" in her proper loud tenor tonation. She was being funny again.

My sister and I giggled, and then we began inching our way toward the back of the house where they always sent us. We were determined to get away before she got her sugar, but did not quite make it.

"Where's my sugar?"

My stomach cringed as I surrendered my face for the big, wet, spit on my cheek.

"Yuck," I said under my breath before I proceeded to the backroom and bathroom sink, my sister beating me there before plopping on the sofa in front of the 18-inch TV.

Our plates would be coming spilling with collard greens with ham hocks, baked chicken and dressing, macaroni loaded with cheddar cheese, pimento potato salad, and home-made lemon pound cake for dessert. She would make sure of it. I hope there is ice cream to go with the cake.

We learned to leave before daddy's finger aimed toward the back. He would slap our behinds if we gave any inkling of being nosey in grown folks business. The routine was clear in the company of adult talk, especially at Aunt Bertha's house. Children go and stay in the back room. Watching the extra-large color television, we chased the big pecan and charcoal long haired cat with amber eyes around the room and under the couch. Lucky him, he sauntered anywhere he wanted to go, tuning in on all the action and conversation with no word of complaint said about his wayward fluffy tail getting in the way.

Skinny legs swinging over the edge of the couch arms watching the *Newlywed Game,* an abrupt pounding of fist shook the wooden door and surrounding wall structure. My sister and I legs stiffened as our eyes found each other. My sister's feet sailed rapidly to the floor as the frantic thunderous knock, now concurrent with yells of "Bertha" shook the surface.

We faced each other with lifted eye brows and scrunched shoulders, saucers for eyeballs for half a second before running to the window to peep. We saw nothing but green sticker bushes and dared not to move out of the backroom where we were. Jumping up and down in frustration after more booms of fist, we second guessed our dad previous qualities for giving a good beating. He had a fierce temper and if we got caught leaving this room we would see it.

My sister shushed me when I started to whine, calling out "momma, momma, I want momma, I'm scared while wringing my hands." A knot formed beneath my belly button.

Through the thin platform walls, Aunt Bertha's high tenor voice began to spew viscous, nasty words I knew and some I didn't know existed. A forceful pop resembling crack wood was heard as if the door gave away and the blare of a tenor screaming made the ruling.

My sister lit out the room with her pony tail flapping. I attempted to stay close on her heels as we whizzed down the hall.

A grating noise like chairs being rearranged, and then a clobber as if something was struck to the floor occurred. Next an apparent blast of shattering glass hurled against the wall widened our eyes as we slowed and tiptoed at the corner to peer in the kitchen. I inhaled as my eyes beheld my dad pressing a 38 against a man's pulsating chest.

"Please Ronnie. Stop this craziness!"

"I will shoot nigga, if you don't leave… now," my dad said.

"Look Ronnie, "my aunts hand resting on his bulging bicep, "I'll see you tonight baby, alone."

"Wit how many others, huh Bert! You just gonna play wit me and den take my money?"

"No Ronnie, you got it all wrong! You drunk man! I will talk to you tonight and explain everything. Come by and we'll talk, I promise love. You know you my baby."

"I'm going this time, but you better be here tonight Bert, you hear!"

The screen door finally shut with a loud thud and my dad spun around to Aunt Bertha, wiping puddles off his forehead, "You need to control your crazy nigga's!"

"I can't help it if they can't get enough of this beautiful Bertha body," she spewed with wiggle of the hips on every syllable and pranced out the room toward the bar. "Woo, I need a big shot of whiskey after this one here! Ronnie's out of control wit' his love for me."

Giggling under our breath we sauntered down the hall, back to the room before dad saw us.

My sister imitated her wiggle into the room that sent me in hysterics.

"See, I told you there will always be action over here."

Later, Mom heard about the incident at Aunt Bertha's from my sister's big mouthpiece. She definitely had a crack in her pot. I believed mother's skin shaded to fiery red with smoke puffs out the ears, but I never saw it. A year passed before our eyes saw the face of Aunt Bertha's.

I overheard the grown folk gossip of the partying cooling down after that night. They claimed Aunt Bertha was seen regularly at church. I was pleased to overhear this.

My aunt could be a great testimony of how God's love can transform. I know her change in behavior would touch a lot of people due to her popularity. No one could deny her drawing effect when in the room, claiming the center of attention. It was time that she lit the room in a positive way, by sharing the Good News of Jesus Christ.

CHAPTER 2

Laughter

For everything there is a season, a time for every activity under heaven.

A time to be born and a time to die. A time to plant and a time to harvest.

A time to kill and a time to heal.A time to tear down and a time to build up.

A time to cry and a time to laugh

Ecclesiastes 3:1-4

WE SHOWED UP in the Scooby Doo van at Aunt Bertha's house a year and some months later. My sister and I were excited to be out of the house, finally! We intended to play Mrs. Pac man or Pole Position all day and eat peanut butter and jelly sandwiches since we could not ride our bikes. The rain drizzled from the tree limbs to fall softly on the grass. My mother left hours earlier for work. We were happy when dad shouted out our names from the kitchen with the command "Go get in the van."

It was warm humid afternoon in May. Our Girl Scout camp was not until later in June so every day we got away from the house was added excitement.

The huge van nicknamed after "Scooby Doo" derived its name from the chocolate and tan brown coloring with deep black tinted windows, and in the back was a bed covered with fuzzyfurry black mattress cover. Tan and black leopard striped curtains were on the back windows. It reminded me of the television cartoon, all spooky, mysterious but comfy. Two seats were in front of the bed, and we could look out the side windows and see everything passing, but no one could see us because of the thickness of the tint.

My older sister disagreed with the van cool appeal. At 13, she was tired of it. Dad made the windows quake with the music Earth, Wind, and Fire till we reached the front of Aunt Bertha's.

We knew it was Aunt Bertha's crib' because Aunt Dessa was just a fourth of a mile up on the opposite side the road. Out we hopped, sprinting up the steps into the front room through the unhooked screen door. We were hungry and hoped there was cooked food or money to go to the corner store for hot dogs and chips. It was quiet as a mouse lurking as dad made his way inside after securing the Scooby Doo Van.

"Bertha," he yelled, "where are you lady with this front door open?"

"Hold on man, I'll be out in just a minute. I'm in the bathroom!"

We galloped down the hall to the back room and plopped into our usual spot. Before we could swing our legs over the arm rest, we heard a boom and felt the floor jiggle, like boulders of rock falling. I thought the roof was opening gazing upward at the ceiling. Seconds later a piercing screech for "help!" filled our confusion and we jolted out the door.

My sister and I dashed back to the front to see what the commotion was. Size eights stopped in mid tracks of the hall and collapse in hysterical laughter from disbelief at the opening of the bathroom. Her glee lead to tear-popping, as her fist pounded the cement floor in hilarity.

I stood trying to absorb the picturesque and not giggle for the first few seconds, but the sight of my aunt reclined on the commode, nearly upside down with her underwear around her ankles and feet angled up in the air was just side splitting. She looked like a roller coaster ride gone haywire, and the situation did not improve with her petite heels flutter kicking in the wind. Her curled locks disarrayed with white rubble and dust framing her body was picture perfect for the National Inquirer. Her tenor voice vehemently spewed curses.

Dad finally dapping to the scene minutes later after me yelped louder after every curse. Finally he managed between deep breaths and gripping his stomach to say, "woman, I told you, you were getting too fat and need to lay off the fried chicken and pound cake!"

Spread eagled next to my sister, we both shook into more convulsions of glee after that comment. Auntie shrilled soprano in anguish, "Ya'll going to call for help for me or what?"

The Lemonade

Aunt Bertha humorous nature was renowned throughout the community. She definitely could and would make anyone squeal with laughter. As I got older, I recognized it more often. I will never forget the day when my dad and I rode to her new home. She moved away from the Seale Road area after that ghastly structure problem with the commode. Rumor was after blasting the owner out she took him to court for bodily damage and negligence and won.

I was in my early twenties now, and down visiting from Atlanta. My Aunt Bertha opened the door and immediately went to the bedroom saying she was in the middle of something.

Dad feeling right at home with no worries, walked directly into the kitchen, calling out, "I don't smell a thing cooking up in here. What else could you have been doing woman?"

My aunt yelled from the bedroom, "Nothing for you. It is my day off and get out of my kitchen. You don't live here, and you show don't volunteer to pay no bills."

Opening the refrigerator, dad scanned until his vision fell upon a pitcher with succulent lemons floating on top.

Hurriedly stretching for a large glass from the overhead cabinet, he proceeded to fill it to the brim. Tipping the glass for a sizable gulp that covered his pencil thin mustache as he dapped to the nearby table, he halted in midskip and reversed. His hairy large hands clutched his throat, as he appeared to give the choking sign in the middle of a three sixty turn. His behavior was as if he took the first puff a cigarette or something, with all his coughing, sputtering while speedily lurching toward the sink. Fluid was heaved out the mouth and nose in eager desperation.

Finally able to take a breath, a screeched sound evoked, "Lady, what is wrong with you, you trying to kill me-ain't no sugar in this doggone lemonade! Woman, how in the hell did you forget the sugar!"

Aunt Bertha waltzed into the kitchen with a full smirk on her red lips, "I see you loved my lemony lemonade."

"Oh, you got jokes, huh?" He continued clutching his throat.

"Man, next time you'll ask before you go into my refrigerator. At this house you drink at your own risk, especially when I am out of sugar. You goin' to the store for me? Anyway you diabetic, so you should have enjoyed it!"

Sitting next to the recovered victim at the table, she gave that famous tenor laugh and said, "Besides, I am sweet enough, all the sugar you need baby."

Aunt Bertha's spiritual lemonade was beginning to formulate. The point in her life where she began familiarizing with the right set of ingredients for a Christ-centered walk. Once again she attended church, singing with the choir and frequently ushered on Sundays. She attempted to clean up her ways but her party spirit cleaved. The doorbell was always ringing with friends bringing bottled gifts that filled the glass and rolled funny cigarettes. They thrived off her jovial fervor and magnetism causing any hermit to bow.

Laughter was effortless to conjure for Aunt Bertha. She probably could get the introvert with zero personality to chuckle if he was around her long enough. But laughter does not mean joy. Aunt Bertha lacked the main ingredient. Joy only comes with true love and relationship with Jesus Christ. Only God can give joy and bring happiness during the time of prosperity and the season of pain and sorrow.

God can bring a smile in personal turmoil such as through the pangs of divorce, deceitful lies such as cyberbullying or just emptiness after loss of a loved one. Even in sickness, like a cancer diagnosis, God can allow someone or something to happen to bring comfort and a smirk. This factor proved true a short time later.

CHAPTER 3

Life

Return, O Lord, deliver me! Oh, save me for Your mercies sake! For in death there is no remembrance of You; in the grave who will give You thanks.

Psalm 6:4-5

AUNT BERTHA WAS in her late-sixties when she became unresponsive in her sleep one night. Rushed by ambulance to the emergency room, the physician reported a thrombosis resulting in stroke that left her weak and impaired in memory and judgment. The stroke severely affected her speech. Slurred syllables and beginning sounds would come out of her mouth when expressing her thoughts and intentions. Difficulty with memory was noticed when she continuously forgot she was in the hospital, often thinking she was visiting someone else. Over time this condition improved, but not enough for her to return to work.

Aunt Bertha during the last ten years remarried, and with his insistence she gave in to resting and taking therapy. In the past both were heavy drinkers and smokers until this awakening. It was challenging step, yet her husband agreed to cease smoking and drinking if she would drop the habits sincerely and focus on her health.

My dad called with the latest news of her condition.

"Mirror, she had to change her whole lifestyle. She is not the same. Even her smile is messed up. She kept talking about how God saved her and seeing a light. I thought I never see the day when Bertha would say, 'Larry, I messed up most of my life. Straighten yours up before it's too late."

"She loves you dad and she doesn't want you sick like her."

He hung up shortly after that comment. I was flabbergasted. Over the phone for the first time in my life, my dad almost seemed fearful with his usual macho attitude. A week later back at home in Phenix City, I was able to see for myself. After being in the hospital for three weeks, Aunt Bertha and I were chatting at her home. Sitting on the side of her bed, her head pressed back on a pillow showing hollowed droopy cheek on the right side of her face. "Mirror, I am glad to see you, dahling. Come give your aunt some sugar."

I leaned over, this time, her kiss was barely wet, hitting the top of my cheek bone.There was no wine, whiskey or rum bottle in sight. Though the house still had a faint cigarette smell, my aunt Bertha never lit up or seems anxious for a cigarette the two hours we were there. She spoke about her close call with death and being scared because there was much she needed to repent.

"Some things I have done; I can't put words to describe them they are so disgraceful.Even the word sin couldn't begin to title it. But God forgives all. I am a new person."

When my dad and I stood up to leave, she reached out and clutched dad's hand.

"You need to stop drinking, gambling, conning and smoking that bud man, You here? Don't be like me. Okay Larry?"

"He knew she was serious because she called him by his first name."

"You still a mess woman, but alright," he chuckled. With his finger pointed toward her, "but only if you stay straight."

She stretched a smile.

We went over to visit Aunt Bertha three months later on Christmas Eve. It was an early chilly afternoon with light frost on the grass. The sky over casted with white and blue gray fluffy clouds, but the day looked promising because we could see the sun light pushing its way through.

Aunt Bertha was mostly recovered and able to work again. She fixed a small luncheon for the holiday for first time since her sickness in lieu of the holiday. A few cousins were over and more people on the way. I joined in on the ride with my dad to her place.

"Heeeyyy!" he said pushing open the unlocked door.

"In here!" she yelled.

He walked right away to the kitchen, uncaring that she could see him from the corner where she was sitting on the bed. She cursed him in the middle of his pimping stride over to her refrigerator.

"Where's the good stuff?"

He began pulling dishes filled with food out from the back of the refrigerator that she had no intentions of sharing. I truly believe, though, she was accustomed to his spoiled nature and glad he still treated her same.

"Now I am going to have to repent for all those words following your name. When you pimp your butt out, put the money for the grocery bill on the table mister for four sides, two meats and dessert."

He chuckled, but kept dishing food onto the plate. He even opened the stove in assurance he had covered all corners.

"And where's my Christmas gift? I didn't see or hear nothing with an engine roll up in the driveway for me. The nerve of you to walk in here empty handed with no shiny ribbon package, not even an envelope!"

"Woman, I'm your Christmas gift!"

"Please! You would be returned back to sender; I wouldn't even shake the box!"

We loved hearing her jokes and how she made my dad chuckle and squirm at the same time.

It was truly a gift.

Two months later, my husband and I paid a visit to my Aunt Bertha that touched my spirit. This time it wasn't a happy occasion. My dad's only brother passed unexpectedly and quickly. He was only in his late forties, left behind were two teenagers, and a wife. We were all filled with a deep pit of pain at the loss. My aunt and I were alone in her room. She asked out of the blue "You and your husband go to church?"

I said "Yes, often.""And you take the baby, right?"

"Yes ma'am."

"Good, I am so glad to hear that 'cause I made a lot of mistakes in my life. I left God out a lot of my life. I don't want you to do the same. I can't go back and fix none of those mistakes or I would, but I have asked God to forgive me for them. Now, if He can just take these stinking cigarettes from me, I'd be doing great. Everything else he has taken away."

She glanced at the pack of cigarettes on the night stand as if to reach out for one and decided against it.

"All those bad habits of partying, smoking dope and snorting, the gambling, and stuff I've let go of. I work, go home and to the church. My husband can testify to that. Baby, don't walk in my footsteps. Walk in the Lord's steps. Don't make the mistakes I did. He forgave me and blessed me with this house and now a new car!"

"Amen Auntie!"

I looked around and could see her artistic skill and flamboyant style marking her personality. A glimpse to the left of the exotic fish tank decorated with bright green, burnt orange and canary yellow patterns, I saw the African fertility masks cradling the bed room walls. But on her nightstand was something I never witnessed until that day. Lying there next to her eyeglasses and cigarette pack lay an opened Bible. I smiled.

Two months too soon after that sad occasion an ambulance rushed her to the hospital again. I recalled those previous words as she lay in Intensive Care Unit at the hospital for two weeks near death. I was at peace if we lost her because I knew she had turned her life around and accepted Jesus Christ as her personal savior.

Death passing over her post, she recovered yet another stroke and went through inpatient rehabilitation for a short period of 6 weeks instead of home health. As the staff and her peers lined up, sad to see her go, of course, Aunt Bertha could not resist her display of comical behavior and boisterous ways before exiting.

"We are going to miss you around here," the nurse said.

"I am going to miss you all too, dahling, but I am glad to go home and eat some real cookin'."

"Well you better come back and see us," giving her a big hug. "We know you will blossom more back in your own surroundings."

"Amen to that, sugar! I love you all" she chimed from the wheelchair as it was rolled out the door.

She walked with a cane the next time I saw her.

"Hello dahling, come give your auntie some sugar."

It hurt her that she could not work or drive. The keys were tucked away safely from her due to her memory deficits. Cooking was also a danger since the day she broke every dish in sight when she couldn't remember how to fix her famous lemon pound cake. Her husband really drew the line when he found her several times with the stove on and she was sleep or on the phone and could not recall she was cooking.

"Hey auntie," and I automatically gave her sugar. She needed some by the sullen look on her face when I walked in the room.

"Let's do a little shopping, okay? I need your help in finding an outfit for a special dinner at work."

"Okay, dahling, but I'll just ride along and show you where to go."

The visit was marked successful after hearing the singing throaty tenor chuckles that flowed as we went down familiar streets. We stopped at all her favorite dress shops.

As the day pressed on, her countenance resembled the old humorous liveliness becoming of her. Her 'Hey dahlings' were back with more tonation and familiar hand gestures. I was overjoyed that the doubtful aunt with the cat's purr I encountered earlier at her home disappeared.

In the ride home, I told her God continues to have a plan for her life, and He kept her here for a reason. I challenged her to be encouraged by drawing on her faith.

"Don't you know that with God, all things are possible? It is only when you don't know Him or step out without Him that you are limited."

She smiled with her gold tooth showing and her eyes glistened over.

The Call

One late morning while sitting at the desk in my office in Decatur Georgia, the phone rung in the middle of typing therapy reports and on the other end of the receiver was the familiar tenor voice. She called my number intending to call someone at the church. This was a repeat performance from two weeks ago but timing wouldn't allow me to accept the call. This time I could speak in length.

"Oh it's you mirror, I meant to call the church dahling, I'm sorry, you okay?"

"I'm great auntie. It's okay, you were destined to talk to me today. So whatcha doing? How are you feeling?"

She began to tell me how useless she felt, and I contradicted and reminded her how useful she still is. We talked for over thirty minutes.

"The days are just boring. I feel like a 90-year-old lady in a shoe. I got to get out and do some things. I can't even go to the church for noon prayer and lunch because they think I will forget how to get there and end up, I guess, at the Russell County police station or in the Chattahoochee River!"

Then she started talking about her previous driving adventures including her trips to my house in Atlanta three years ago.

"You remember I cooked that year because I had to doctor your sick pitiful turkey."

The whole crew including my dad and mom were at my house in Decatur Georgia along with uncles, aunts, and cousins. It was a great time.

Everyone found somewhere to lay his or her head that night in our home. Until dawn we made side jokes and gestures, watched movies, and played video games. Pizza and ice cream splurges replaced the empty dishes of Thanksgiving dinner. Squealing children bored with stuffing and exploited turkey quietened as they shoved sausage and pepperoni pizzas down their mouths. Before the day ended, we went out to get a paper and to see who beheld the best Black Friday sales.

Aunt Bertha was determined to be at all the red eye and early bird specials. No one else made a sound to agree when she voiced her intentions earlier in the day.

My Aunt Dessa loudly stated "Leave me out of this sale stuff, I don't want to get up and fight through no lines and half deranged and sleep deprived people at the crack of dawn for anything."

A conversation thirty minutes later revealed Aunt Dessa had been reeled in with wit and threats and red circular lines could be seen all over her preferred ads. Half sleep on the couch with butter pecan residue on the tip of my tongue, I grinned with closed eyelids at their amusing interchange. Startling me with slap on the thigh, I screeched in painful jargon from biting my tongue as they informed me I was chauffeuring.

Now alert, I nicely interjected, "Only if someone is going to knock me out of bed with a broom to wake up on time."

They chimed snidely in hummingbird harmony, "that can be arranged with no problem sweetheart!"

We shopped half the day, and when the time reached 2:00 P.M. I was beyond exhausted driving from north to south Atlanta looking for sales. Both aunts were too beat to keep me awake as I inched in the driveway with one eye open. All I heard was synonymous piping nasal sounds as I looked back at the two with drools and their head bobbed backward on the seat.

Aunt Bertha ability to encourage people to go along with her convictions was almost infallible. She managed to bring humor in play while swaying decisions with precision.

Realizing it was time for me to utilize my techniques, I convinced her during those thirty minutes on the phone to address some of her personal goals.

"Aunt Bertha what about those days you would flap your hands in frustration over disorganization at your house and stated if you had more time things would change. All those creative plans of rearranging furniture and switching color schemes. Remember the samples that are to this day lying in one of your drawers."

"I did say that, but I can't even drive. Not even to go to the church that's less than five miles away- nowhere! I get tired just washing a few dishes! I'm just useless now...," her voice dragging the final consonant.

"Aunt Bertha, why don't you let the pastor or deacons know at the church you want to participate in the out-reach programs and afternoon prayer? I am sure someone will arrange for you to be picked up some kind of way. Ya'll appear to have an active ministry, and I know they are concerned about you from the many food plates and flowers brought over to your house. You get phone calls every day!"

"Yeah, Maybe I'll mention it to some of my choir members who are coming over today."

"And remember Auntie, you don't have to do every-thing in one day. Start small like if you want to change the way your pictures hang on the walls and sit on the tables- set that as the goal for the day and switch a few in one room. Progress counts small steps in the right direction."

With a lift in her voice, "Thanks dahling, I love you- now I gotta go and get ready for my company. I'll call you later."

CHAPTER 4

Love

Love is patient, love is kind. It does not envy, it does not boast, it is not proud. It does not dishonor others, it is not self-seeking, it is not easily angered; it keeps no record of wrongs.

I Corinthians 13:4-5

MY AUNT BERTHA thrived on shopping for the latest and greatest clothing and shoe styles. I remember visiting her one fall evening while in town from Atlanta.

She was talking and walking hurriedly. Rambling on and on about her big event that night and rushed into that huge walk-in closet of hers to show me what she was going to wear. There were shoes in boxes on every side and at the tip top of her shelves. Three levels of clothing were on one side and two levels on the other displaying all her flamboyant styles.

While she was digging for the "must see" gown, Auntie chattered on about the banquet where she would be one of the honorees. It was a community organization I was unaware she was a partner of, and she was due to be recognized for dedication and over achievement of service to help others.

"Wow, Aunt Bertha, this is a great honor! Don't forget to have pictures made."

"Oh yes, they are going to have a photographer there and the news people. I'm also getting honored with a plaque."

Aunt Bertha was forever opening her doors before her illness to take in others, bringing food to the elderly and sick, donating her clothing, and making time to take people to the store, doctor, or other necessary appointments.

"It's about time someone recognize this big ol' heart of mine."

I giggled as she begins to prance with the gown held to her in the mirror. It was good to see her smiling and joking again.

"Do you see your Auntie? She is going to be a knock out in this!"

She gave me one of her big famous wet kisses on the cheek as she hurried to grab the matching shoes and purse.

Auntie was back to her typical self except for the occasional slur in words, and she used the cane for steadiness outside the home. Her memory was fine for long term and familiar routines but for short term she covered her refrigerator with To Do Lists and bedroom with a huge calendar marked with appointments. She continued to forget things on the stove without a reminder, so they stopped her completely from cooking while alone. But she appeared to be joyful and bright.

Memories

The end of life came for my Aunt Bertha sooner then what we all expected. She was progressing well, we thought, and began walking without a cane for short distances outside the home.

Most felt as if she was back to her old self with the funny jokes and some light cooking, which she loved to do. She returned to attending church regularly because her endurance increased for activities. The choir rejoiced at her visits back at rehearsals, and missionary team welcomed back her expertise with the activities with the food bank and assisting the elderly. Everything appeared to be improving and on the upswing to wellness.

I received a call early one Friday morning from my dad. His voice barely above a whisper shared, "Uncle C' came home from an overnight shift at work and called Aunt Bertha's name as he walked into the room. When he came close enough to touch her, he knew she was not with us anymore. She went peaceably," he croaked.

I sat down in the middle of the unswept kitchen floor, dropping the broom. My ears could not stop replaying the words over repetitively "Aunt Bertha is dead." I knew

I needed to go home immediately. The following day I left for Phenix City.

The weekend I drove home. The trip appeared to be longer than usual. There was an overcast in the sky. I saw no sun bursting through the cloud cover to light the atmosphere. My shoulders slumped further down as I pass the Chattahoochee River crossing into Phenix City from Columbus.

At my mother's house, I rested back onto the familiar colorful cushions of the couch with a long exasperated breath and a glass of thinking sweet tea, "Momma, I just don't want to remember her this way."

"I understand, and you don't have to," as she sat and brought her arms around me to lean back on her chest. "Focus on the good times and cherish them because that is not her in that coffin, it's all your decision, but I think your dad would like the support."

In my momma's arms, I wept for my friend and aunt who not only lit up the town, but also brightened and melted the hardest of hearts with her vibrant spirit and love.

I did not attend the funeral as desired. Thankfully, I could honestly use the excuse of skipping the occasion due to starting a job less than a month before she died. The funeral was arranged to be in the middle of the week.

As I was driving down the familiar 280 by pass out of Phenix City, observing old spots and shops. I recollected on her qualities missing the joyous, confident, empathetic, hardworking, joking and loving Aunt Bertha. The diva with the loud high tenor pitched voice who came to know the person of Jesus Christ. She shared Him with me, and I believe she spoke with others how "He is before all things, and in Him all things hold together (Colossians 1:17)."

Many days passed and I find my thoughts gravitating to her, especially during the Thanksgiving holiday when I return home to Phenix City, Alabama, cruising along the 280 Bypass. US Route 280 is a spur of US highway 80 that travel along rural towns and the smaller cities of Georgia.

As I drive by the stores on the bypass of 280, the memories return of how we couldn't go anywhere without somebody shouting "Hey Bertha!"

She gave her usual big smile as they walked up with her common reply, "Hey dahling" and on to the jokes. Later on she would say sitting in the car "I don't know who that was, Oh my God!"

I would raise my eyebrows at her in disbelief, because usually she stood holding a conversation with them for at least fifteen minutes. Asking about their mom, job and offering an uplifting word in a joking way. They would have no clue she did not remember them.

A giggle come forth out of my lips thinking along those happy memories, and the sadness evaporates. I turn the knob on the radio and sing out elated knowing that she accepted willfully the gift available to her. The gift offered of salvation. That alone brought me peace not only for her, but for my dad also, who passed on two years later. He too opened his heart to accepting Jesus Christ. God does answer prayer.

CHAPTER 5

DURING MY FINAL visit with Aunt Bertha, a touching story was shared from a revival church service she attended. The story was about a young man who stepped onto an elevator with another gentleman to the 10th floor of a medical building downtown.

This other gentleman was an elderly 93-year-old who walked upright with a straight cane, yet had the youthful appearance of a man ten years younger. Both were going to the same floor where the pulmonologist department was located.

The elevator opened, then closed, and began to ascend. Within seconds of the doors closing and upward movement of the elevator, the elevator jerked and lights flashed on the inside. They came to a halt between floors. Minutes passed and nothing happened, and both came to the realization it might be a moment until the elevator move again.

"I'm calling emergency," the young man said.

He picked up the red phone hanging behind the enclosed glass and tried to reach someone in emergency services. A silence was the only result of his efforts. Slamming the receiver back in place, the elderly man glanced in the young man's direction, and then slid to sit on the floor. His head rested back upon the cool metal.

The young man continued standing, shifting his from one foot to another, wringing his hands back and forth. The elderly man glanced his way, dropping his chin he closed his eyes.

"How can you be so calm?" the young guy finally said and eased down on to his bottom to rest back against the corner of the elevator. His frustration clear in every syllable.

"I have learned that in life things happen for a reason and for the good of them who love the Lord and are called for His purpose. So I let God drive, and I ride."

Chuckling, "Oh, you on that Holy roll thing. Pops, Look, I have given up on that Godthing. If there was a God, I wouldn't have the lump the size of a golf ball on my lung right now, and I've never smoked a cigarette in my life!"

"Son, I am 93 years old, and I can tell you there is a great God. I too had a lump on my lung the size of a golf ball. I was cured at 33."

Lifting one eyebrow, the young man replied, "Hey that is how old I am." Pausing, he stuttered, "So what are you doing here if you are cured? And what do you mean by cured?"

"Son, I mean all signs of cancer have vanished from the lobes of the lung and my bronchioles."

"Then what are you doing here if you are cured?"

"For you son, if you can open your heart to believe it. I was at the diner across the street having breakfast and was about to walk my three blocks home when the Holy Spirit told me to come here and get on this here elevator and wait. Since the day I received healing in this very same, now renovated building sixty years ago, I have given my life to God. I have walked through fires and not been burned, rode many highways and not been injured, flown many places and came back unharmed. I'm not saying it's been rosy, there were many hardships and losses of loved ones, yet God needed me all for this moment. (You see, the elderly man was a retired fireman). Are you ready to receive your deliverance and healing?"

The younger man looked at the silver haired man with his deeply etched lines flowing along his forehead and a frosty white haired chin. He peered into his warm brown pupils searching for some sign displaying weakness and dishonesty. He felt a pulling inside; a desire that this was his time, but still there was a miniscule of doubt lingering.

"Why are you joking with me Pops? You expect me to believe that you are stuck on this elevator because of me. I guess it quit working so we may have this chummy chat too, huh? Come on, Pops, you are pulling my leg."

"Son, I don't joke about the power of God. The question is do you want to be healed?"

You see, before him was not just a wrinkly elderly man in disheveled clothing but a prophet filled with the Holy Spirit of the Lord giving him a chance at life as led by the Spirit. He paused, a wrinkle coming across his forehead, his eyelids half closed to tighten and lips curled shut in thought of what to say. Shaking his head as if to clear his disbelief; he gazed directly into the old man pupils, again searching for any uncertainty.

"Yes," he responded, coming to kneel on his knees. "Yes."

Eyes moist, remembering his wife and newborn baby at home, he bowed his head.The prophet whispered with a tender voice, "Only God give second chances, and yours is here, if you believe."

Faith

Aunt Bertha believed healing and faith would bring her to wellness. What is faith and how does one get healing? Faith is explained by this passage in Galatians 2:20:

> "I have been crucified with Christ and I no longer live, but Christ lives in me. The life I now live in the body, I live by faith in the Son of God, who loved me and gave himself for me."

With faith in God, we grow to believe as Hebrews 11: 1 states, "Now faith is confidence in what we hope for and assurance about what we do not see."

Aunt Bertha's faith in the Son of God brought hope that He would hear her prayer for healing of her body. Allowing this hope to manifest, unlocks the door for answered prayer. Because Aunt Bertha was confident, the hope lever was pulled and due to this faith healing became established. I am confident God answered her prayers and she walked within a healed whole body before she took her final rest.

Aunt Bertha cleaned and was mobile around her home without a walker or cane the last month of her life. Her speech improved where she communicated without slurred words. Her conversations revealed clear articulate thoughts and intentions without long pauses which led to her returning to favorite daily tasks, such as cooking and organizing.

She knew the restoration of her body. The answered prayers sent up to Heaven interceding on her behalf. Faith gave her joy in those last days and peace with her final breath.

CHAPTER 6

THE WORD OF God can transform. According to Merriam Webster dictionary, transform means to change in composition and structure, outward appearance, character or condition. It is a word of action and activity, not passivity.

There is someone, whether relative or friend who you can relate to Bertha's testimony. Remember, the growth that took place in my aunt's life came from accepting and developing a relationship with Jesus Christ. Unfortunately, before her walk of becoming a Christ-centered person, she participated in some activities that pleased the flesh and affected her health in a negative way.

Most of us have and maybe still are participating in sinful acts that satisfy self and pleasure the flesh. We avoid Christ-centered living and guidance. The difference in making mistakes is to learn and grow, mature with the realization of knowing there is more that exists than we;

> "For the Word of God is living and active; sharper than any double-edged sword, it penetrates even to dividing soul and spirit, joints and marrow; it judges the thoughts and attitudes of the heart. Nothing in all creation is hidden from God's sight. Everything is uncovered and lay bare before the eyes of Him to whom we must give account (Hebrews 4:12-13)."

There is nothing passive about the Word of God; the works of God, and what He expects of us. Isaiah 51:6 says,

> "Lift up your eyes to the sky, then look to the earth beneath; For the sky will vanish like smoke, And the earth will wear out like a garment And its inhabitants will die in like manner; But My salvation will be forever, And My righteousness will not wane."

The Testimony

Aunt Bertha shared her spiritual lemonade with others. What she gained through growth in God, manifested through her light, life, laughter, and love to many that knew her. The weekend of her funeral revealed great evidence in how often she shared faith and hope in Jesus.

One after the other, friends, family and associates admitted in conversation how she talked about Christ to him or her. Frequently, most disclosed the conversations usually came up during unusual events such as house parties, basketball games and even in front of the liquor store. All joyfully admitted her earnestness stirred something on the inside of them.

Bertha was bold about her faith. She would say thangs such as "I know you need a change in your life, you been doin' this too long, I'm here for you and bringing Jesus, hold on to us and He'll make us all strong." One woman spoke as she reclined on the sofa at my Aunt Dessa's house.

"I remember the last time I saw Bertha, I told her to come over for a drink, I had our usual bottle waiting, and some bud to smoke. I took out the table so we could even play a round of poker. All of us was shocked because she wasn't having it. She came over, didn't lift a glass of liquor to her lips or hold a smoke, but during laughter and jokes turned my party into a testimony service and invited everyone there to church."

People saw the change that took place, they witnessed the difference in her reactions and responses and many said they wanted that change that affected her to infect them.

Maybe there has been stagnation in areas of your life? A division in some important relationships, such as with husband or wife, children, grandchildren, mother, father, or even a close friend. Perhaps there is a financial strain tightening with no bars to release and improve, no doors opening, no light shining in a dark and desperate situation.

Now is the time to sit, reflect, meditate and get a revelation. Whose path or direction have you been following?

What leadership were you taking your direction from? Is there any presence of Jesus Christ in your life?

My best friend that I love and trust is my freckled face shorty named Tyler. We have been friends a very long time. It all started a very long time ago in Elementary school. He loved to talk about God and what the Kingdom might be like. It was weirded out for such a shorty as he. Not cool at all.

But Tyler's gift is his ability to speak to anyone about the Word of God and tell his story. His favorite verse in the Bible is "I am not ashamed of the Gospel of Jesus Christ, for it is the power of God to salvation for everyone who believes. Rom 1:16 (NASB)" He brings out the best of Jesus in me. It started one spring afternoon when he shared his story of what happened in a small city church three blocks away.

"You know; I use to worship the Devil."

This was the beginning of our first conversation on the swings during outside break.

I graced him with squinting brown eyes and a crinkled nose. My shoulders turned toward the other guys next to me hoping he would go away and I began to spin in the swing.

"I did," he interjected with his body blocking the daylight so I would look at him squarely in the crooked pudgy nose. "I worshipped the Devil until a miracle happened. You believe in real life miracles don't you?"

I stopped moving the swing in circles and said, "I'll be the judge of that; I'm listening."

"Okay, one night we were coming from having Pizza J's, our bellies all full of pepperoni with triple cheese. My sister and I began throwing "you ugly jokes" at each other. The parents weren't paying attention because their mouths were too busy passing pokes at each other under their breaths about how my dad kept cutting his eyes at the waitress. They always thought we didn't understand so we acted clueless.

My father, as usual, passed the barn looking white church with a high steeple cross on the roof. It was our sign that we were going the correct way home. That odd wooden church appeared to be the only light in the dark starless sky. Except this night, it was as if the steeple was filled with Christmas lights. And guess what, at the tip top was that plain maple wood cross. And what was weird is that, this night it seemed to give off all glittery colors of red, greens, purples and even diamond spurts like fireworks. I almost slapped myself to make sure I wasn't seeing things from being high off sugary soda and chocolate chip M&M cookies.

Suddenly, my father growled a nasty word in anguish and his grip tightened on the wheel attempting to keep it straight. The Old Ford wasn't responding so the grunts became shouted curses as he yanked the wheel of the Ford Expedition. We began to veer off to the right and into the entrance of the winter white wooden church, half full gravel parking lot. Dad hit the brakes and the tires screeched to a halt as we slid into two parking spots just missing another Ford truck and some other cars. I was glad we didn't end up in the ditch or something! Then the engine died. We all took a breath than began yelling at once.

Dad hollered 'Please, just shut up everyone!"

He turned the ignition key again, and nothing happened.

Mom pulled out the cell phone to call someone, but there was no signal. Lifting her head, dad shook his head before mom could ask and then pushed open the car door. Mom pushed hers open and stood up. Both seem to exhale and drop their shoulders together when their eyes fell upon the church doors.

Knocking on the window, Dad signaled us to come on.

"Looks like we're going to church."

"Dad are we going to have to be here long, I wailed?"

"Son, as long as it takes to get us some help. Sit at the very back."

Tip toeing into the half-filled, dimly lit room, we quietly slipped in and sat on the right back row, all four of us hunched together as if we were in a horror movie instead of church. No one said anything to us but smiled and there was a middle aged bald man who showed all his teeth and passed us four programs with notes on them. The preacher was on the stage speaking with the Bible open.

Tyler suddenly jumped off the swing and started walking, moving around our swings in circles as he kept speaking. His hands started arching and turning at the wrist.

The pastor spoke for a short time and then began getting excited. He spoke about someone named Gideon boldness with leading an army when he was a small man and not a warrior, and then about Timothy was timid, but God changed him into a bold preacher and teacher.

He said that Jesus, God's Son was sent to save us and would make our lives change if we just believe. That He makes the impossible-possible. Something began to happen within me when the preacher started shouting 'Jesus' and moving about the stage left and right. I got the urge deep in my gut to shout 'Jesus' too! But I didn't. Instead I burped and scooted closer to my sister.

Every time the preacher moved and dance speaking that name 'Jesus' I squirmed, and held tight to the pew seat. My sister turned to me, raising her eyebrows while mouthing 'what?'

"Jesus! Jesus! Jesus!"

Shouted repetitively in a high tenor by the preacher, he commenced to dancing down the steps of the stage and jumping up and down. My sister quickly forgot about me and the question.

Turning my head back to her, I shoved her for no reason and my sister eyes remained glued to the preacher. She didn't even waste a blink on me.

Leaning forward to peer at mom and dad was my next move. Mom kept crossing and uncrossing her legs. Popping his knuckles, dad seemed to be rattled, switching from one hand to another.

"J..e..s..u..s…!"

The preacher screeched again, holding each letter as a musical note.

My heart filled with song. A wave of static electricity pierced my body and traveled to my toes. The lady in front hopped to her feet. Unaware of how I got there, I was bouncing on my size eight high top shoes echoing 'Jesus' too. Tears came down my face as I leaped up and down like a firecracker. That fire hasn't stop burning since.

"What happened to your mom and dad? Did they look at you funny? I would have."

My swing stilled slowly while awaiting Tyler's answer.

"The preacher took them and had them hold hands and he prayed till my mom eyes start to water. My dad's lips even trembled. Then they called us over and put oil on our foreheads. It was weird but great! A warmth came over me and my sister told me later she felt like she was getting a great big hug, but didn't see anyone.

Riding home later, my dad folded his hands over moms and even brought them to his lips while whistling a song. No one mentioned that the car started right up when the switch was turned and dad turned the steering wheel easily with one hand. The man from the church just smiled as if it was not a surprise and waved us away with a blessing. I pressed my face against the window looking back as we were pulling away, he nodded toward me grinning, holding the jumper cables in both hands."

"Wow Tyler, what a story!"

"It's not a story, but the truth. Now don't you want to know about this 'Jesus' who made me leap from the seat to my feet in joy?"

And that's how our friendship began...

I recall a time at my previous church when the pastor shared with the congregation what God pressed on his heart.

"I was given the word that there is a great need for the church to reach outward with fervor and love to the surrounding and neighboring community. Programs of reading and tutoring services, food and clothing banks, and finance classes are needed. We have to help the people of this community and be a spotlight for God. Our light isn't shining!"

The church membership openly accepted the dynamic vision, and suggested additional programs such as visiting the nursing home, delivery of clothing and food boxes for shut ins, a banking ministry, and neighborhood evangelism once a month.

A date for posting signup sheets was set to spur things into the right direction. The pastor asked everyone to meditate on the focal points and ministry direction established on that day.

"I am asking you to pray and ask God for direction as to what service areas God leads you to assist, if any. When lead by the Spirit, sign up for one or more of these ministries because faithful workers are necessary for these challenging new programs to be a success," he proclaimed from the pulpit.

After one month of the pastoral leaders of the committees speaking and asking for the church to pray about Godly direction on the outreaches, the signup sheets was posted to no avail. Very few people added their signatures. Several months of meetings, committees were not able to be cohesive about decisions. Scheduled programs routinely were cancelled and enthusiasm dwindled. Numerous attacks of sickness and death went through the congregation. Degrading rumors and relational conflicts magnified between members.

One morning after ending a meeting with the head of all committees and not getting anywhere with decisions and the vision, the pastor collapsed to his knees, falling upon his face in despair in his small office. His head bowed in defeat and despair, he cried out "What is wrong, my God? Please help me! You gave me this vision and nothing is happening!"

He heard a firm yet gentle inward voice declare, "You finally asked."

The pastor called a revival. Persistent prayers and teaching focused on reconciliation to God and forgiveness. For three months, he took each topical subject and dissected for study beginning with Salvation, Repentance, Reconciliation, Restoration, and Faith and the church became on fire for God. Members began confessing aabout disagreements amongst themselves, and strained relationships were reestablished. Visitors from the nearby neighborhoods began coming into service and giving their lives to Christ. Spiritual revival brought a renewed relationship in the Church. The pastor reintroduced the vision for the community programs with success for outreach and evangelism.

Reconciliation is to restore friendship and harmony. Reconciliation explained in detail in I Corinthians 5:17-21states:

> "Therefore, if anyone is in Christ, he is a new creation; the old has gone, the new has come! All this is from God, who reconciled us to himself through Christ and gave us the ministry of reconciliation: that God was reconciling the world to himself in Christ, not counting men's sins against them.
>
> And he has committed to us the message of reconciliation. We are therefore Christ's ambassadors, as though God were making his appeal through us. We implore you on Christ's behalf: Be reconciled to God. God made Him who had no sin to be sin for us, so that in Him we might become the righteousness of God."

A Charge

We are on this earth for the purpose of Loving God and loving others. Matthew 28:19- 20 reads,

> "All authority in heaven and on earth has been given to me. Therefore go and make disciples of all nations, baptizing them in the name of the Father and of the Son and of the Holy Spirit, and teaching them to obey everything I have commanded you. And surely I am with you always, to the very end of the age."

Love is our responsibiity. The Bible in Mark 12:28-31 explains,

> "One of the teachers of the law came and heard them debating. Noticing that Jesus had given them a good answer, he asked him, "Of all the commandments, which is the most important?"
>
> "The most important one," answered Jesus, "is this; 'Hear, O Israel: The Lord our God, the Lord is one. Love the Lord your God with all your heart and with all your soul and with all your mind and with all your strength.' The second is this: 'Love your neighbor as yourself.' There is no commandment greater than these."

Love gives light. Light cannot be contained but spreads through the darkness and the coldest of places to produce warmth and growth. Love is not easy. Over time love can grow and mature. Love does not inflict pain or bring a person to shame. Instead, love gives, and not takes, and causes increase, instead of decrease. When nothing else works or reaches to the inner core of a person, love can.

Let your light shine and give off love that overflows to help others to recognize, accept and establish a relationship with the greatest love of all...Jesus Christ.

If you do not know this love, please know and believe that God loves you by reading with me John 3:16-21:

> For God so loved the world that he gave his one and only Son, that whoever believes in him shall not perish but have eternal life. For God did not send his Son into the world to condemn the world, but to save the world through him.
>
> Whoever believes in him is not condemned, but whoever does not believe stands condemned already because they have not believed in the name of God's one and only Son. This is the verdict: Light has come into the world, but people loved darkness instead of light because their deeds were evil.
>
> Everyone who does evil hates the light, and will not come into the light for fear that their deeds will be exposed. But whoever lives by the truth comes into the light, so that it may be seen plainly that what they have done has been done in the sight of God.

In Him I Can Stand

In Him I can stand with my back straight.
Hold my head up, look someone in the eye and say,
"I am somebody!" He takes away the pain-
the sorrow and disdain-
Removed are the addictive habits that swallow desires
to see the sunlight of tomorrow.
He is larger than my problems
and helps me face the dew of
the morning, Because He
is my Lord and Savior,
my precious Lamb and Conqueror.

Worthy is He to be praised!

When I can't get up because my mind and heart are so
heavy with despair; my worries fill my gut with hate and
my food can't digest so I regurgitate;
The insides of my head pound like waves against the seashore,
and sleep is something I wish for; My taste buds crave for
cigarettes, alcohol, and mind controlling drugs to ease reality;
And my feet can do nothing but make the floor boards
sing and think of mortality...

I don't care if I wash, eat, dress to work. If I live-
wouldn't care If I die!

Halleluiah for ... He Cares. He Lives
He welcomes. He Loves.
Open up and inhale His Living Word for He is life. Faith
for overcoming all and
Hope to live.

Nothing can lift one higher and keep them filled than
the Fountain of Life. Worthy is the Lamb to be praised
I say, Praises to the Worthy Lamb!

LaMuriel Yvonne Ojo

mirrorbuzz99@gmail.com.

www.ingramcontent.com/pod-product-compliance
Lightning Source LLC
Chambersburg PA
CBHW060714030426
42337CB00017B/2861

9780985597832